For Joyce — with Love — Jan. 1, 1982

! Happy New Year !

(see especially pp. 184-5)

May your year be joyous,

XXX X

Jerelle — and Ezra Stone

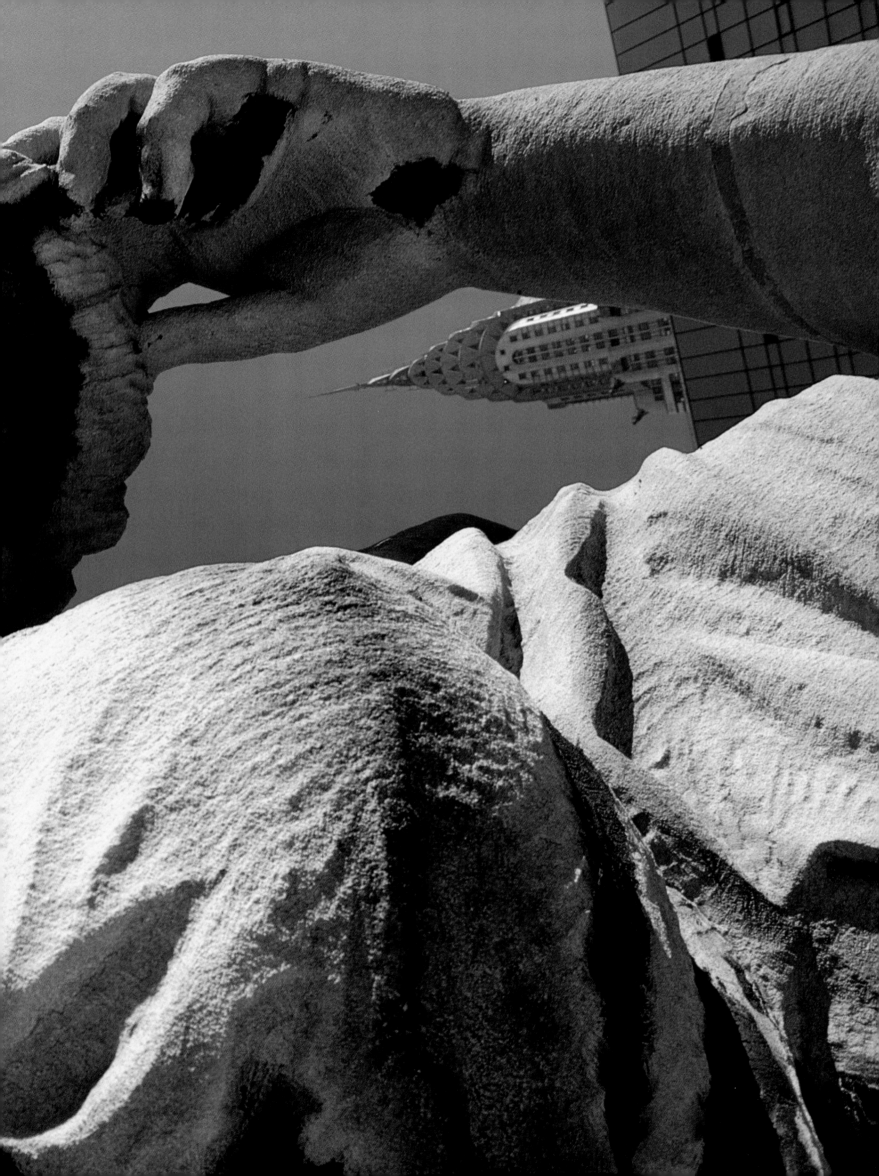

The O

YONAH S

KNIS

AIR CONDITIONED

TAKE HOME SOME OF OUR
COCKTAIL KNISHES

Potato or Kasha

LIVER PUFFS

FRANKS in JACKETS

OUR FAMOUS
Apple Strudel
EAT IT HERE OR
TAKE SOME HOME

riginal

HIMMEL

HERY

COOKIES
MUHN
KICHLACH

POPPY
FLAVOR

ONAH'S
ATONICK
HOLE OR
LICED
E ONE HOME

Recommended in
The Lower East Side
Shopping
Guide

Est
1910

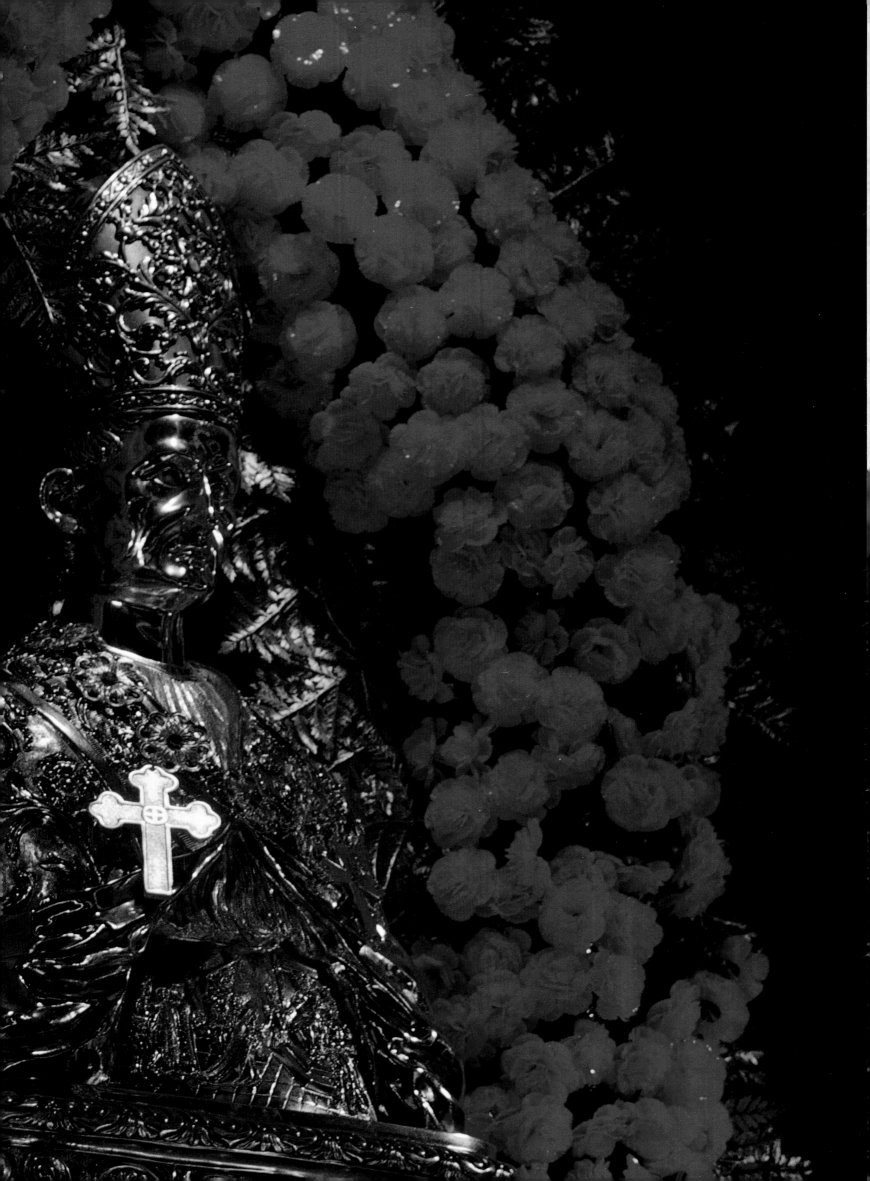

Designed and with an Introduction by
Jean-Claude Suarès

Text by
Chris Casson Madden

Assistant Photo Editor, Research and Permissions
Deborah Augenblick

Photographs by

Bob Adelman
Mariette Pathy Allen
John E. Barrett
Bill Binzen
Paolo Buggiani
Sonja Bullaty
Langdon Clay
Jan Cobb
Jere Cockrell
Chris Collins
Hugues Colson
Henry Cox
Henri Dauman
Bob Day
Charles E. Dorris
Timothy Eagan
Paul Elson
Bill Farrell
Cal Fentress
Enrico Ferorelli
Mitchell Funk
Michael George
Aram Gesar
Diego Goldberg
Dudley Gray
Stephen Green-Armytage
Ernst Haas
Serge Hambourg
Jim Hamilton
Laszlo Hege
Ken Heyman

Walter Iooss, Jr.
Mark Ivins
Armen Kachaturian
Peter B. Kaplan
Ted Kaufman
Thomas A. Kelly
Brian Lav
Susan Lazarus
Angelo Lomeo
Jay Maisel
Stephanie L. Marcus
John McGrail
Michael Melford
Roy Morsch
Margery Motzkin
Eleni Mylonas
Marvin E. Newman
Ruth Orkin
Jon Ortner
Toshi Otsuki
Jean-Pierre Pappis
Jeff Perkell
Lorenzo D. Perrone
Jake Rajs
John Scheiber
Jane Schreibman
Frank Spinelli
Joseph G. Standart
Joseph Vasta
Charles Wiesenhahn
Tom Zimberoff

Harry N. Abrams, Inc., *Publishers*, New York

MANH

CONTENTS

*36–41   July 4th fireworks light up
Manhattan's skies as seen from Brooklyn
(Jay Maisel)*

ATTAN

1 A cast-iron Manhattan manhole cover that is on its way to becoming an endangered species since this particular model is no longer being made (Laszlo Hege)

2–3 Peeking over the wing of a Boeing 707 as it approaches New York's LaGuardia Airport. The Twin Towers of the World Trade Center with one hundred ten stories are the highest points in Manhattan (Ted Kaufman)

4–5 Over twenty shops and restaurants line the three-tiered Citicorp market in the base of the Citicorp Building at Lexington Avenue and 53rd Street. The multilevel atrium was opened in 1978 and also houses four stories of offices besides the market (Henri Dauman)

6–7 An unorthodox view of the Chrysler Building as seen from the statue of Athena, goddess of civilization, part of Jules Coutan's sculpture on top of Grand Central Terminal's southern facade (Peter B. Kaplan)

8–9 The cast of Stephen Sondheim's Sweeney Todd, taping an "I Love New York" commercial for television. This particular segment was filmed at the South Street Seaport in downtown Manhattan on the square rigger The Peking (Roy Morsch)

10–11 A wall in a lower East Side playground pays homage to graffiti—a controversial New York "art form" (Diego Goldberg)

12–13 Evening light on the lower East Side looking toward Brooklyn. The Manhattan Bridge, built by Carrère and Hastings in 1909, is in the background on the left next to its more famous sister, the Brooklyn Bridge (Charles E. Dorris)

14–15 The East Penthouse Suite in the New York Hilton Hotel on Sixth Avenue in midtown. This nine-room duplex, featuring a circular staircase, antique chandeliers from a Russian church, and a Yamaha piano among other comforts, commands a nightly fee of fifteen hundred dollars plus one hundred twenty dollars for New York's sales tax (John McGrail)

16–17 Paolo Buggiani, an artist who works with the elements of nature—earth, water, and fire—climbed sixty feet up a rope extending from one of the television antennas atop the World Trade Center's Towers and, with some kerosene and a cigarette lighter, spit fire above Manhattan. Self-portrait by Paolo Buggiani entitled "Unsuccessful Attack by Paolo Buggiani"

18–19 City Tunnel No. 3 still under construction. This water tunnel is thirteen miles long, begins in the Bronx, travels through Manhattan under Amsterdam Avenue until 102nd Street, then veers east, and at 78th Street heads toward the East River and Roosevelt Island. It is lined in cement and is eight hundred feet deep at its lowest point (Peter B. Kaplan)

20–21 The cream-colored concrete exterior of Frank Lloyd Wright's Solomon R. Guggenheim Museum, completed in 1959 at Fifth Avenue and 89th Street (Jan Cobb)

22–23 One of the monks in the domed top of the Islamic Center at 1 Riverside Drive reads a book by morning light while the flotilla of "Tall Ships" on the Hudson River during the 1976 Bicentennial celebration passes beneath him (Walter Iooss, Jr.)

24–25 Avenue of the Americas, known more prosaically to most New Yorkers as Sixth Avenue, at 2:00 P.M. on a normal workday. Over 700,000 cars enter Manhattan below 60th Street each day (Walter Iooss, Jr.)

26–27 A fourth-generation knishery on East Houston Street on the lower East Side, Yonah Schimmel, is open seven days a week and is famous for its potato and kasha knishes (Bob Adelman)

28–29 Patrons feast on a suckling pig at Number One, a Chinese restaurant on Canal Street in Chinatown. The area is a magnet for visitors and New Yorkers alike, with its more than two hundred restaurants (Paul Elson)

30–31 Early dawn illuminates the Twin Towers of the World Trade Center as pre-rush-hour traffic makes its way across the Brooklyn Bridge (Peter B. Kaplan)

32–33 Each September 17th, Mulberry Street (also known as Via San Gennaro) is the scene of the Italians' festive San Gennaro celebration. This silver-and-brass statue of San Gennaro is paraded with a marching band to its temporary shrine at the corner of Hester and Mulberry Streets (Charles E. Dorris)

INTRODUCTION

"I stood spellbound as I saw that building in that storm. I had watched the structure in the course of its erection, but somehow it had never occurred to me to photograph it in the course of its evolution. But that particular snowy day, with the streets of Madison Square all covered with snow, fresh snow, I suddenly saw the Flatiron Building as I had never seen it before. It looked, from where I stood, as if it were moving toward me like the bow of a monster ocean steamer, a picture of the new America which was still in the making" (Alfred Stieglitz referring to the Flatiron Building, 1902–1903).

Manhattan, the City of the Future, was the first to usher in the twentieth century. It was once a city expanding in all directions with the help of the most envied transportation system in the world including elevated train tracks and steam locomotives. And yet the past generation has witnessed Manhattan's failure to keep up with the twentieth century. The failure of that very same transportation system and the population explosion have turned Manhattan into an island again, cut off from its neighbors by outdated bridges over two wide rivers, constant traffic jams that stretch for miles, expensive parking spaces, and a nearly bankrupt subway system. But Manhattan has never stopped growing. The worst of times has witnessed countless structures springing up and dwarfing other structures that just a few years before had been considered The Tallest In The World. Manhattan, an island of constant changes, improvements, and surprises, functions in its own time frame, its own hectic pace, incomprehensible and frightening to those who inhabit its physical and spiritual confines and even more to those who visit it.

On September 27, 1839, less than six months after the *New York Observer* published a letter from Samuel F. B. Morse, the inventor and painter, describing Daguerre's successful experiments in Paris, an Englishman named D. W. Seager exhibited the first daguerreotype ever taken in America: an outdoor view of Manhattan. It showed St. Paul's Chapel with its surrounding fields and two-story houses, with a glimpse of the Astor House. By the 1850s photographers had begun documenting Manhattan's people and streets. There were nearly a hundred daguerreotype galleries in Manhattan specializing in "likenesses" and just as many amateurs lugging their equipment through the streets and fields of the island. Studio photographers of the day managed to lure every important businessman, general, and opera singer to sit motionless in front of the camera, while outside it seems that every palatial home, every government building, and every sailing ship in the harbor was captured on a glass negative. One daguerreotype gallery, on the corner of Fulton Street and Broadway catty-corner across Barnum's Museum, belonged to Mathew B. Brady, the famous photographer of Abraham Lincoln and of the Civil War. Brady found Broadway changing faster than ever after the war and helped record Manhattan's leap into the future.

Inevitably Manhattan has held an immense attraction for every generation of serious photographers, photoreporters, and visitors with cameras. It is impossible to remember Manhattan in any other terms than the dozens of great photographs that are so deeply impressed on our minds... Jacob Riis and members of the Society of Amateur Photographers immortalized "the other half's" life in the poor tenements of the 1890s before the whole area was torn down. Alfred Stieglitz's photograph of the Flatiron Building remains the standard image of the turn-of-the-century push for the skies, while Paul Strand's *Looking Down* of 1922 is a perfect complement to it.

George Grosz, Double-Decker. In 1932 Grosz recorded his first impressions of New York with a camera. Unlike his drawings and paintings, he opted for a record of the atmosphere instead of concentrating on the specific.

Walker Evans's street scenes and building fronts, and Berenice Abbott's stores and skyscrapers, not only document the 1930s but also give a deep sense of the decade. And is there a more charming record of post-World-War-II class consciousness than Weegee's candid photographs of uptown society confronted by midtown riffraff?

"I longed to arrest all beauty that came before me, and at length the longing has been satisfied" (Julia Margaret Cameron).

This is not a guidebook to Manhattan. Such books have already been done. There are guidebooks to the streets, structures, events, children's activities, complete-guide-books-with-maps, guidebooks-to-the-best-of-this-and-the-best-of-that, and they come in twenty-three languages. Instead, this book is an attempt to catch a sense of the city's overwhelming size and vitality, the crushing density of its crowds, the continuous transformation, all through contemporary color photography. It is an attempt to gather a collection of photographs that form an immediate feeling for Manhattan's identity, photographs that should confirm and enlarge our own vision of that city, that describe not through a series of streets and buildings but with a collage of unexpected themes. The seventeen themes that make up this collection emerged through careful editing of thousands of images supplied by

George Grosz, Shoeshine, *1932. Grosz was not interested in faces or events, only in a sense of place and feeling for the times.*

48

nearly one hundred photographers. (Some themes, however, were contributed entirely by one or two.) It seems that every photographer working in Manhattan has at one time or another pointed his camera directly at the sky and caught a strange configuration of passing clouds, or pointed it down toward the street below to record an abstract form created by passing crowds and vehicles. After nearly a hundred years of posing for pictures, the Brooklyn Bridge is still photographed every day. So, it seems, are the Chrysler Building, the Empire State Building, and the World Trade Center. Every season in New York lends itself to photographic essays, but winter steals the show. What other island can boast of the serenity of Central Park and the chaos of Second Avenue?

It is surprising to find that more than one photographer has caught the same subject. What is even more surprising is that quite often the same subject has been caught by several people at the same time of day and from the same angle. Such was the case with several photographs of reflections. It seems as if some puddles with the Empire State Building's reflection have hired press agents. If one were to pick the most patient subject the award would go to the horses of New York. They've been posing for over a century without a fee or a complaint.

For once, the camera has been turned on the tourists who are themselves armed with cameras. The result is a look at those who come here to look. Speed, the by-product of an impatient city, results in the most frantic chapter, while the chapter on how sunlight hits New York points out that, isolated or not, Manhattan is part of a larger world, infallible in some respects, but still vulnerable to the moods of the seasons, the weather, and the times of day.

There has always been ample proof that photographers made a pact a long time ago to document the city. This book is proof that it is a deeper commitment than ever thought possible before. Their task has been not only to describe every physical detail but even more to give a sense of life during special times. Faced with an era of constant contradictions, they have managed to sort out the vital and the irrelevant, the triumphant and the bankrupt. They have paid homage to Manhattan. This book is an homage to them.

J. C. Suarès
Manhattan, March 1981

LOOKING UP

In a city where pedestrian survival hinges on split-second reflexes and peripheral vision to avoid speeding bicyclists, zigzagging garment racks, and the imminent dangers of the fastest walkers in the world, New Yorkers rarely take a moment to look above ground level.

When they do, the effect can be breathtaking.

Manhattan's uplifting pleasures range from the barrel-vaulted ceiling of Grand Central Terminal, with its magnificent expanse of zodiac constellations, to the dizzying effect of looking up at the Twin Towers of the World Trade Center from street level where one can almost imagine that Manhattan is spinning. Even the ceiling in the men's smoking room in the New Amsterdam Theater is worth the price of admission. Manhattan—full of vertical surprises.

a

b

c

50 *a. The domed ceiling of the men's smoking room of the New Amsterdam Theater on West 42nd Street (Armen Kachaturian)*

b. A bank's oval stained-glass skylight (Charles Wiesenhahn)

c. The sky-lit dome of the Solomon R. Guggenheim Museum, upper Fifth Avenue (Jake Rajs)

51 *Dubbed the Flatiron Building because of its resemblance to the household appliance, this twenty-one-story structure reigns supreme over the once fashionable splendor of Madison Square Park. The three-sided building was designed by architect Daniel H. Burnham (Mitchell Funk)*

52–53 *Karl Bitter's statue Abundance stands in the center of the Pulitzer Memorial Fountain, built in 1915 by Carrère and Hastings in front of the Plaza Hotel on Fifth Avenue. It is used as a backdrop for many fashion advertisements and commercials (Bob Day)*

54–55 *"Underdog" floats above the city streets during the annual Macy's Thanksgiving Day Parade, which winds down Central Park West and Broadway to Macy's Department Store on Herald Square at 34th Street (John Scheiber)*

56   Looking skyward at the clock on the
Helmsley Building (originally the New
York Central Building) at Park Avenue and
45th Street. Real-estate tycoon Harry
Helmsley refurbished the building in 1978,
and had gold leaf applied to Edward
McCartan's clock and sculpture of Ceres
and Mercury (Peter B. Kaplan)

57   Surrounded by the skyscrapers of
Rockefeller Center, the recently gilded
Prometheus *majestically surveys the
sunken plaza in front of the RCA Building
(Peter B. Kaplan)*

58–59   *The old and new merge on 53rd
Street between Fifth and Sixth Avenues.
The ABC Building towers on the left and
part of the Museum of American Folk Art
can be seen on the right (Jeff Perkell)*

60–61   *Ivan Chermayeff's giant red* Nine
*of the Solow Building at 9 West 57th Street
looms in the foreground (Michael Melford)*

62   A subway rider's view emerging from
the BMT station at Broadway and 23rd
Street (John McGrail)

63   The elegance of an older New York's
Plaza Hotel, vintage 1907, contrasts
sharply with its new neighbor on West
58th Street, the sloping glass facade of
the Solow Building, completed in 1974
(Chris Collins)

64   Looking up at the statue of George
Washington by John Q. A. Ward on Wall
Street. It was completed in 1883 at the
exact site where Washington took the oath
of office in 1789 as first president of the
United States (John Scheiber)

65   Two hundred fifty thousand light
bulbs illuminate the trees surrounding the
Tavern-on-the-Green Restaurant in Central
Park each Christmas. This remodeled
restaurant overlooks the Sheep Meadow
(Peter B. Kaplan)

66–67   A view from the center strip of
Park Avenue in midtown Manhattan,
encompassing, clockwise from upper left,
the Banker's Trust Building, the Union
Carbide Building, New York General
Building, the Pan Am Building,
the American Brands Inc. Building, the
Chemical Bank Building, the Westvaco
Building, and the Waldorf-Astoria Hotel
(Jake Rajs)

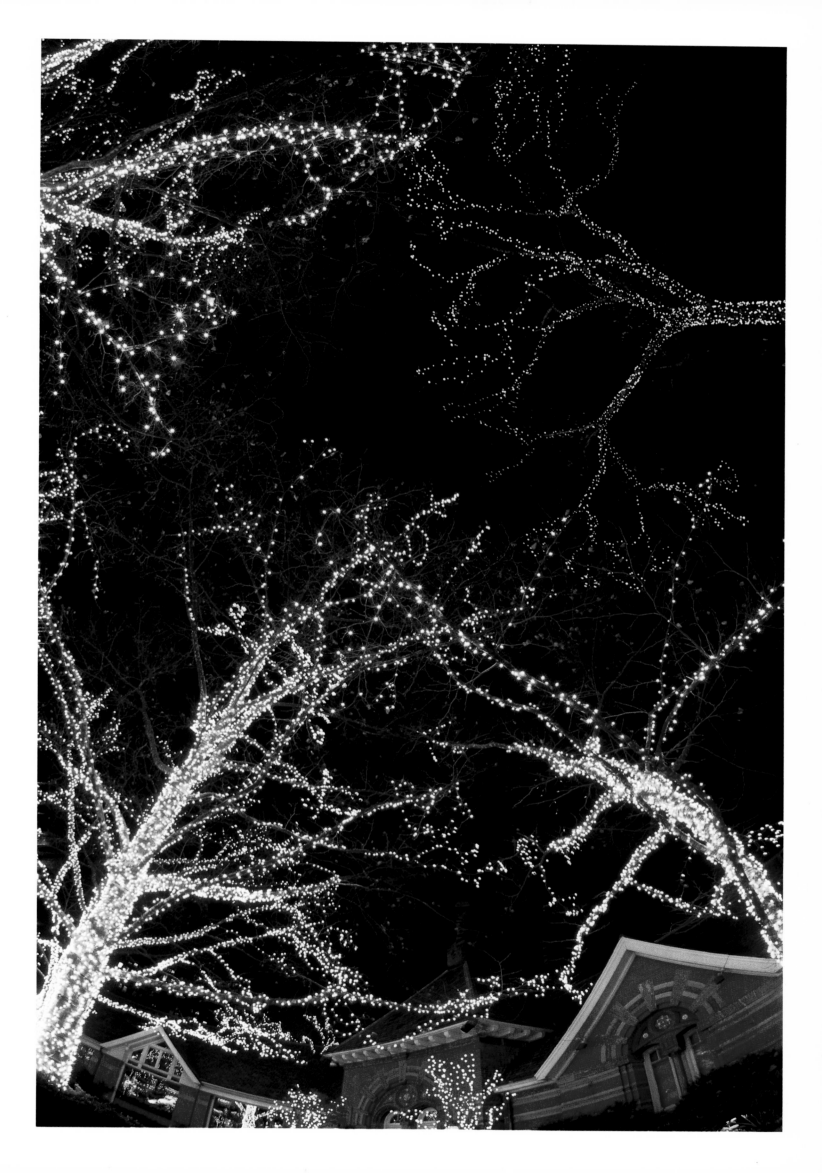

BIG CLOCKS

a

b

Manhattan is the one place in the world where one can keep track of the time without wearing a watch.

Clocks are everywhere. Big, small, digital, antique, and, in uniquely New York fashion, the only clock in America imbedded in a sidewalk (on Broadway at Maiden Lane in lower Manhattan).

New Yorkers can see clocks from nearly every vantage point in the city. At the zoo, in subways and train stations, and housed atop some of Manhattan's fine older buildings, including the Paramount, the Consolidated Edison Building, and Saint Paul's Chapel.

As Paul Kugler, Manhattan's most notable timekeeper, who is responsible for keeping some of the biggest clocks in this city ticking (including the clock atop Grand Central Terminal), sentimentalizes: "You can't have a favorite clock in this business. All the others would get jealous."

68   a. Paul Kugler has spent over twenty-five years as timekeeper of the Grand Central Terminal clock (Peter B. Kaplan)
b. The digital clock at 127 John Street in lower Manhattan—an urban oddity in New York's financial district (Sonja Bullaty)

69   The clock on the northern facade of Grand Central Terminal suggests the grandeur that Warren & Wetmore and Reed & Stem created in 1913 when they designed Grand Central (Peter B. Kaplan)

70   Workmen repair the clock once touted as "the largest four-dial clock in the world," which sits three hundred fifty feet

up the front of the Metropolitan Life Insurance Company Headquarters at Madison Avenue between 23rd and 25th Streets (Peter B. Kaplan)

71   Originally the third Judicial District (or Jefferson Market) Courthouse at Sixth Avenue and 10th Street, this Vaux & Withers building was saved in 1967 only through the extraordinary efforts of Greenwich Village residents and is now the Jefferson Market Branch of the New York Public Library (Peter B. Kaplan)

72   The clock on the tower of the Paramount Building at 1501 Broadway, which was at one time owned by

Paramount Pictures. Its famous theater was once housed in the first six stories of the building (Peter B. Kaplan)

73   Since 1853 H. F. Metzer's Atlas Clock has guarded the door of Tiffany & Company stores, traveling uptown with the growing city from 550 Broadway to Union Square, to 37th Street and Fifth Avenue, and finally to the main Tiffany Building at 57th Street and Fifth Avenue. The wooden figure, which is nine feet tall, has solid lead feet and is coated with bronze to withstand the New York climate (Peter B. Kaplan)

74   This four-faced clock, set above the
information booth at Grand Central
Terminal, is the official timepiece for one
hundred eighty thousand commuters and
five hundred thousand people who pass
through the station each day (Sonja
Bullaty and Angelo Lomeo)

75   Designated an official New York City
landmark, the clock atop the Consolidated
Edison Building at Irving Place and 14th
Street was completed in 1926. The clock's
tower was designed by Warren & Wetmore,
architects of Grand Central Terminal
(Peter B. Kaplan)

76–77   The Toy Center of the USA at
200 Fifth Avenue, double exposed with
the Metropolitan Life Tower clock on
Christmas Eve (Frank Spinelli)

HORSES

a

b

c

Horses have always been a major ingredient in the fabric of Manhattan. In the nineteenth century, the city depended on thousands of horses to maintain its daily life and the horse became an indispensable animal, used for such tasks as cleaning streets, pulling fire trucks, ambulances, and the carriages of the Disinfecting Corps of New York's Health Department, which distributed disinfectant in its struggle against cholera.

The Bull's Head Horse Market, near Fifth Avenue and 46th Street, and the American Horse Exchange on Broadway at 50th Street were the scenes of frequent horse auctions in the late 1800s. The constant use and occasional abuse of horses by city residents prompted Henry Bergh in 1865 to found the Society for the Prevention of Cruelty to Animals.

Although twentieth-century New York has seen a decline in the horse population, horses still are much in evidence in modern-day Manhattan, but now they are used usually for pleasure. A permanent tribute to this animal can be seen throughout the city in the surprising number of equestrian statues, ranging from Augustus Saint-Gaudens' statue of General Sherman to the Monument to Peace donated by Yugoslavia to the United Nations.

78   *a. General José Martí by Anna Hyatt Huntington at Central Park South and Sixth Avenue (Langdon Clay)*
    b. Joan of Arc by Anna Hyatt Huntington at 93rd Street and Riverside Drive (Aram Gesar)
    c. General Sherman by Augustus Saint-Gaudens at Fifth Avenue and 59th Street (Aram Gesar)

79   *A well-known literary watering hole on Hudson Street in Greenwich Village, the White Horse Tavern has been in existence since 1880. One of its most famous habitués was the poet Dylan Thomas (Mark Ivins)*

80 Pieces of art glass are imbedded in the wooden carousel horse, circa 1890, in the window of the Sideshow Shop on Ninth Avenue and 23rd Street (Mark Ivins)

81   One of the wooden horses on the
Michael Friedsam Memorial Carousel,
which was erected in 1951 in Central Park,
replacing an earlier one destroyed by fire
(Lorenzo D. Perrone)

82 *St. Patrick's Day bunting drapes*
one of the old hansom-cab horses at
the southern entrance to Central Park
(Ernst Haas)

83 *An aging veteran of the hansom cab*
tourist route through Central Park in front
of the Plaza Hotel at Fifth Avenue and
59th Street (Serge Hambourg)

84 Troop A's stables at the First Precinct
Stationhouse are home for twenty-one
police horses. Built in 1905, it is cleaned
daily by city employees called civilian
hostlers (Serge Hambourg) ...

85 ...And over on 38th Street on the
West Side the hardworking Central Park
hansom-cab horses live in somewhat
shabbier circumstances (Sonja Bullaty)

86 *An oasis in the city's urban sprawl,*
Central Park's lush springtime (Sonja
Bullaty)...

87   ...And sometimes gentle snowstorms
create a bucolic setting for horse and rider
(Sonja Bullaty)

88–89   Dogs meet horses on Columbus
Avenue in the nineties (Serge Hambourg)

SUNLIGHT

a

b

Manhattan's sun is different from other suns. It rises up in a city that is already awake, already in motion. Unlike the rising of the sun in the country or the suburbs, New York's morning sunshine is not a universal signal for all of its citizens to rouse themselves from sleep and get ready for a day's work. For some it's a sign that the night's revelry has drawn to a close or that their night's work in a restaurant, apartment building, or hospital is over.

This is not to say that the sunshine in New York goes unnoticed. Quite the contrary. Stand on the corner of Fifth Avenue and 60th Street in early spring and watch New Yorkers bask in the first warmth of the bright spring sun as it splashes the southern end of Central Park and the square in front of the Plaza Hotel. Wander past the docks that dot the western boundary of Greenwich Village on the Hudson River as sunbathers warm themselves in the scorching August sunshine.

New York's hardiest sun worshipers flock to the rooftops of the city's apartment buildings to create, from early spring to late autumn, what Manhattanites caustically refer to as "tar beach."

90   a. *A winter afternoon sun on Fifth Avenue and 54th Street (Henry Cox)*
     b. *A ceramic tile mural in Greenwich Village near Bleecker Street (Joe Standart)*

91   *Isamu Noguchi's perfectly balanced sculpture, made with ½" aluminum plate, stands unwaveringly on the plaza of the Marine Midland Bank Building at 140 Broadway (Michael George)*

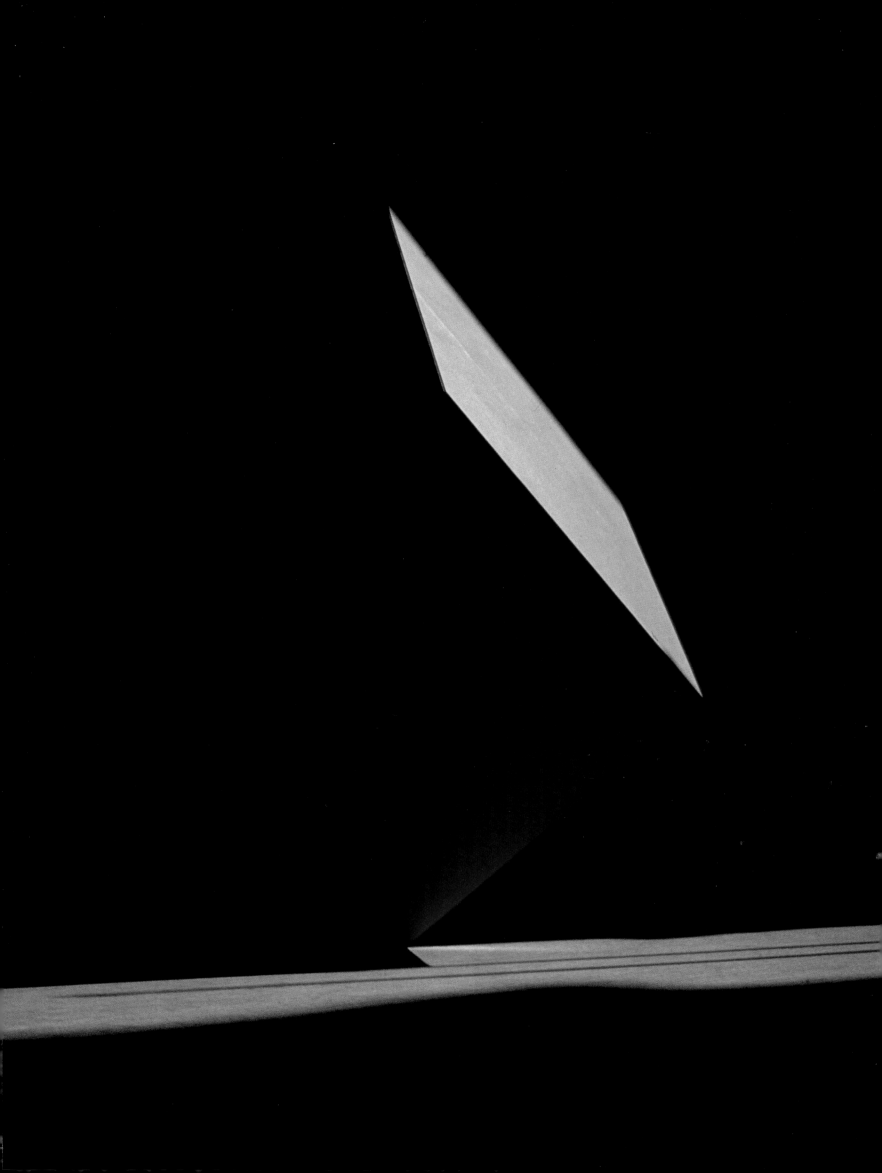

92   With a backdrop of the jagged skyline
of lower Manhattan, the Twin Towers of the
World Trade Center glisten as the sun hits
New York harbor (Jay Maisel)

93   Late-afternoon sun illuminates the
one-thousand-two-hundred-fifty-foot tower
of the Empire State Building (Ernst Haas)

94–95   Looking west on 23rd Street on a
sunny autumn afternoon (Dudley Gray)

96–97   High-noon sunlight floods the
bar of McSorley's Old Ale House at 15 East
7th Street. The oldest saloon in New York
City bowed to modern times on August 10,
1970, when women were finally admitted,
but vestiges of old New York saloons, such
as no cash register, still remain (Mark
Ivins)

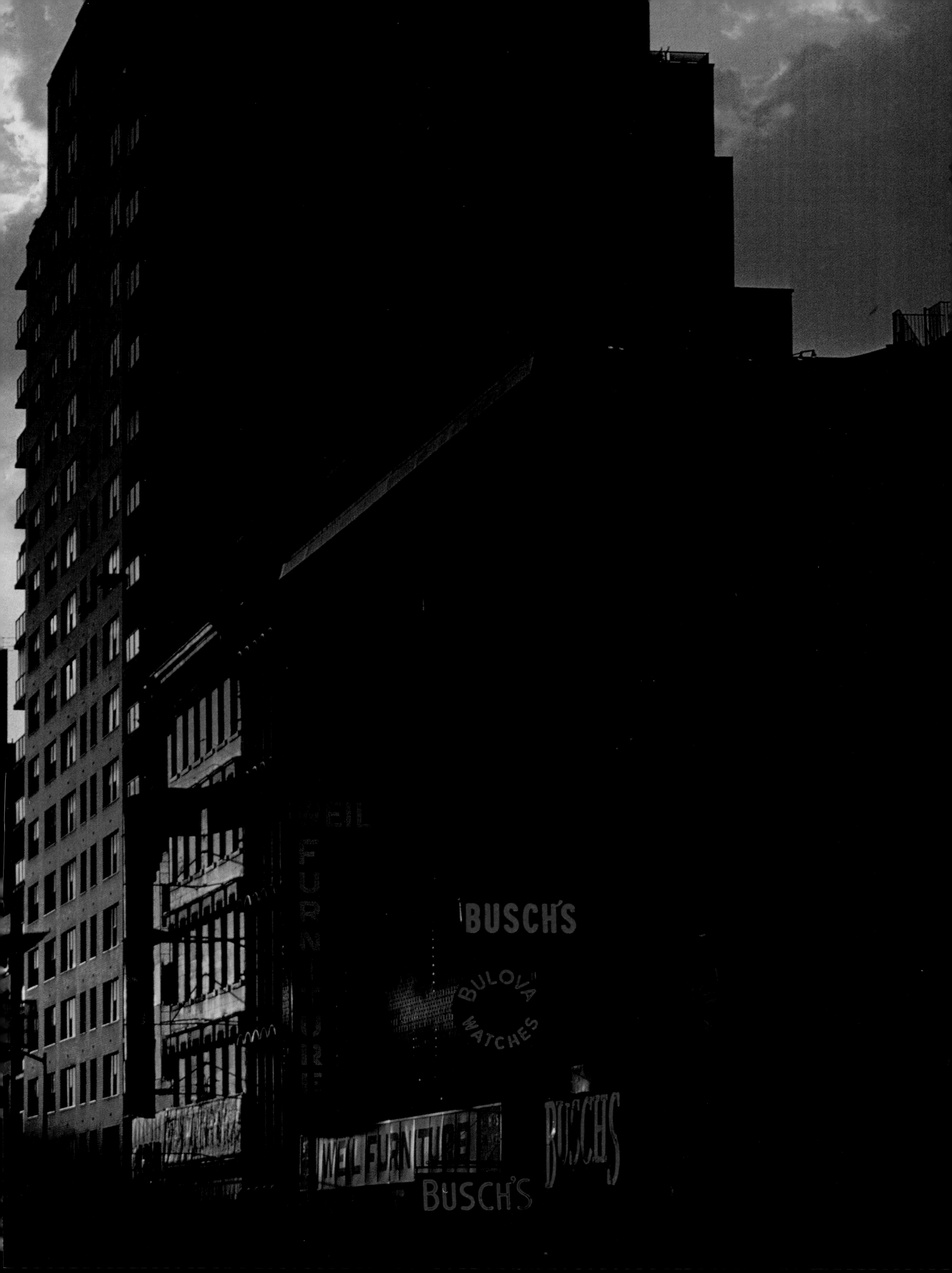
BUSCH'S
BULOVA WATCHES
BUSCH'S

98   *A blizzard of ticker tape on lower
Broadway. A traditional New York
welcome, the ticker-tape parade is
supposed to have been originated by Grover
Whelan in 1919, when the Prince of Wales
visited the US for the first time. When
Charles Lindbergh paraded down
Broadway, several tons of paper rained on
the streets of New York City (Jay Maisel)*

99   *Laundry hanging out to dry in the
rear of tenements on the lower East Side
at 10th Street and Avenue A. For most
immigrants arriving in New York in the
nineteenth century, the tenement was in all
likelihood their first home (Bill Binzen)*

100–101   *Early morning sunlight on
Schermerhorn Row, now part of the South
Street Seaport. This historic landmark
area has the only remaining group of
Federal and Greek Revival commercial
buildings in the city (John Scheiber)*

*102   The awning at 953 Fifth Avenue
shelters the doorman from the early
summer sun (Timothy Eagan)*

*103   Jim Mahan, the doorman at the
Elizabeth Arden Salon for the last fifteen
years, welcomes a bright morning. A day
of beauty behind the Red Door at Arden's
costs one hundred ten dollars (Serge
Hambourg)*

104　An employee of the Lily Lake Cheese
Company at 347 Greenwich Street, the
original butter-and-cheese market in the
city, faces the noonday sun (Susan
Lazarus)

105　A woman basks in the early morning
light by the entrance of the New York Stock
Exchange, which opened at 8 Broad Street
in 1903 (Hugues Colson)

106   *Even the most remote canyons of this*
skyscraper-studded city catch the rays of
the afternoon sun, which accentuate the
multitude of colors that make up the urban
landscape (Dudley Gray)

107   *The sun casts an uninterrupted*
reddish glow along 42nd Street—one of
the few East-West thoroughfares in the city.
The view is outside Grand Central
Terminal (Ted Kaufman)

FACELIFTS

Manhattan is a city always in need of a refurbishing, a cleaning, a touching-up. The very vastness of this town doesn't permit a full and complete cleaning. As one structure is scrubbed, such as Saint Patrick's Cathedral, another needs to be tended to. A bridge must be repainted, a building must be gutted and rebuilt, and another skyscraper must be steam-cleaned to eradicate the ravages of urban grime and pollution.

Manhattan's multitude of workers all tell the story of the city's facelifts—a face speckled with paint, a construction worker wearing the uniform bright yellow hat, one precariously cleaning a building, and another with even more courage painting a bridge. It's the city of the eternal facelift.

108   The paint-spattered face of a worker on the Williamsburg Bridge. The bridge, with a span of one thousand six hundred feet, was completed in 1903 and was designed by Leffert L. Buck (Peter B. Kaplan)

109   Most of New York City's bridges are in a constant state of refurbishment. A surefooted worker paints his way across the giant cable of the Manhattan Bridge (Peter B. Kaplan)

110   The front window of Mahal, a
northern Indian restaurant on Lexington
Avenue and 28th Street, gets finishing
touches before its opening in the spring of
1980 (Henry Cox)

111   *A steady hand in the Bowery (Bill
Binzen)*

112–113   *One of the final steps in the
refurbishment of the Helmsley Building
at Park Avenue and 45th Street was the
steam-cleaning of Ceres, goddess of
agriculture (Peter B. Kaplan)*

114   The national colors of Italy—red, white, and green—give new life to the Third Avenue tenement that houses Ray Bari's Pizza Parlor in its ground floor (Henri Dauman)

115   It took sixteen months, starting in 1978, to give St. Patrick's Cathedral at Fifth Avenue and 51st Street a complete exterior cleaning. Here, workmen scrub down the stained-glass rose window, designed by the Morgan Brothers, which stands between the two octagonal spires (Peter B. Kaplan)

116–117   A backdrop for many movies, from Dead End *in 1937 to Woody Allen's* Manhattan *in 1979, the Queensboro (or 59th Street) Bridge receives another coat of the sixty thousand gallons required to paint it (Peter B. Kaplan)*

118–119   Oblivious to the rumble of Park Avenue traffic beneath him, a workman applies a final coat of gold leaf to the renovated Helmsley Building (Peter B. Kaplan)

PEAKS

a

b

A view that most street-bound New Yorkers seldom, if ever, experience is the spectacular, albeit smorgasbord, world that exists atop the city's towers and skyscrapers. It is not the elevation of these buildings alone that dazzles; it's the elaborate, occasionally exotic, details and architectural one-upmanship that mesmerize its audiences. They range from the Chrysler Building, with its automobile icons, stainless-steel arches, and radiator-cap gargoyles, to the contemporary sensibilities of the Citicorp Building's solar roof.

The skyscraper phenomenon really began in 1893 with the construction of the Manhattan Life Assurance Building. It was followed in 1902 by the Flatiron Building, which catapulted an unbelievable—in its time—twenty-one stories over Manhattan and which for many years symbolized the new age of skyscrapers. The city's skyline continued to soar as Cass Gilbert's Gothic Woolworth Tower rose sixty stories above lower Broadway in 1913. The Chrysler Building and 40 Wall Street vied in 1929 for the title of the world's tallest building, with the Chrysler Building winning out with its one-hundred-eighty-five-foot spire.

The battle continues today with midtown a frenzy of new construction that will once again change the Manhattan skyline.

120 a. One of the Twin Towers of the World Trade Center as seen from its other tower (Peter B. Kaplan)

b. The Chrysler Building on the left and the Empire State Building on the right appear through the window of the offices of the Eastman Kodak Company on Sixth Avenue (Peter B. Kaplan)

121 Foley Square is the seat of most municipal government activities in New York. It houses, among other buildings, 15 Park Row, which has the two dome tops in the foreground, with the US Court House on the left and the Municipal Building on the right (Michael George)

122 Soaring one thousand forty-eight feet into the New York dusk, the Chrysler Building's Art Deco tower was one of the first to make extensive use of stainless steel (Peter B. Kaplan)

123 Citicorp Center, built in 1977, is the third tallest building in midtown Manhattan and its most dramatic feature is its sloping peak—one hundred thirty feet of smooth aluminum atop a nine-hundred-foot tower. The trapezoidal roof, which faces south, originally was designed to use solar energy (Jake Rajs)

124 Downtown in Foley Square, the US Court House. This twenty-story tower, designed in 1936 by Cass Gilbert and Cass Gilbert, Jr., is surmounted by a gilt pyramidal cap (Henri Dauman)

125 Standing six hundred twenty-five feet above Park Avenue at 50th Street are the towers of the Waldorf-Astoria Hotel. This hotel, with one thousand eight hundred rooms, houses apartments in its two towers (Henri Dauman)

126 The fifty-nine-story Pan Am Building hides the thirty-five-story Helmsley Building in mid-Manhattan. At one time a heliport, the landing pad is now unused after an accident in 1977.

127 The Excelsior Hotel on West 81st Street near Central Park West has sixteen floors of hotel rooms (Jeff Perkell)

128 A close-up of the tower of the Municipal Building in lower Manhattan. Adolph A. Weinman's statue, Civic Virtue, resides atop the ten-story tower, which rests on the twenty-four-story building (Henri Dauman)

129 The Empire State Building, its summit cutting into the sky, was built in 1931 by the firm of Shreve, Lamb & Harmon (Timothy Eagan)

WINTER

a

b

c

The world-famous Michelin *Green Guide to New York City* notes simply: "Although quite cold in winter (often around 32 degrees Fahrenheit), New York's climate is fairly dry and brisk. The sky is usually a clear bright blue, which may suddenly be covered over with clouds bearing a rain or snowstorm, snarling traffic temporarily."

New Yorkers will probably grant the Michelin *Guide* the benefit of an understatement in describing the city's sometimes trying winters. The chilling winds of Manhattan can often create temperatures well below the 32 degrees mentioned above, and New York snowstorms are capable of crippling this city which prides itself on its ability to surmount all civic crises—from transit strikes and blackouts to mad bombers.

For the most part, New Yorkers seem to enjoy the major snowstorms that throw the city into a brief turmoil each winter. Sometimes, as in 1888 and in 1960, the storms are of epic proportions and do, indeed, paralyze New York. But for the most part, winter blizzards are a chance to cross-country ski down Park Avenue, to build funny-looking snowmen in Washington Square Park, or to look around at a city silenced and blanketed in white.

130 *a. Rockefeller Center's Prometheus, done in 1934 by Paul Manship, oversees the Promenade Café in summer... (Serge Hambourg)*

b. ... and ice skaters in winter (Serge Hambourg)

c. Aristide Maillol's bronze sculpture languishes on a snowy afternoon in the sculpture garden of the Museum of Modern Art, at 11 West 53rd Street (Sonja Bullaty)

131 *Twenty-one stories above 23rd Street, where Fifth Avenue and Broadway meet, the Flatiron Building, originally the Fuller Building and completed in 1902, reigns elegantly over Madison Square and*

retains the glamour that made it once the city's most famous skyscraper (Dudley Gray)

132–133 *The lower-Manhattan skyline assumes a frigid arctic appearance. New York's cold winters occasionally produce ice floes on the Hudson River (Peter B. Kaplan)*

134–135 *The aftermath of the blizzard of 1978, which immobilized the city. Residents of Prince Street on the western border of the Soho district cope with the snow (Susan Lazarus)*

136–137 *Normally bustling Park Avenue is stilled by the 1978 snowstorm. A limousine waits across the street from the Waldorf-Astoria Hotel at 50th Street (Jay Maisel)*

138–139 *A gutted 653–655 Broadway in downtown New York, formerly housing the Tele Star Instrument Corporation. The building typified the cast-iron style, which predominates in New York's Soho district (Dudley Gray)*

*140   Olmsted and Vaux's designs for
Central Park included gently winding
paths and pedestrian walks, cast-iron
bridges, and ornamental brick archways
(Jon Ortner)*

141   In 1873 Emma Stebbins, who was
the sister of the then Parks Commissioner
Henry Stebbins, created Angel of the
Waters. It stands in the center of the
Bethesda Fountain in Central Park,
reigning over the four cherubs—Purity,
Health, Temperance, and Peace (Toshi
Otsuki)

142–143   The first snowfall in Central
Park's Sheep Meadow after seventeen acres
of much-needed sod was put down in
1980. The entire Sheep Meadow measures
twenty-five acres and before it was used
for concerts, softball games, and soccer
matches, sheep actually grazed there
(Jon Ortner)

144–145   Christmas lights and snow at
Tavern-on-the-Green in Central Park near
67th Street. This recently renovated
restaurant was built around Central Park's
1870 sheepfold (Ruth Orkin)

*146   A woman feeding pigeons on the
east side of Central Park. Besides the
ubiquitous pigeon, some two hundred fifty-
nine species of birds have been sighted in
the park (Timothy Eagan)*

*147   Normally traffic-laden Seventh
Avenue belongs to the pedestrians in
the aftermath of the 1978 blizzard
(Walter Iooss, Jr.)*

146

CROWDS

New Yorkers are renowned for their individuality and independence. The legend that most Manhattan apartment dwellers don't know their next-door neighbors is widespread and probably for the most part true. What is also true, however, is that the urban environment often compels city dwellers to gather in a concentration of crowds—small and sometimes quite large.

Witness Bloomingdale's at 1:00 on a Saturday afternoon as a solid phalanx crowds Lexington Avenue at 59th Street near the department store's entrance; or the lines found almost anytime outside a first-run movie theater in Manhattan. Some crowds are festive, like those found waiting at the bar for the next table at Elaine's; and some are not so festive, like the throngs waiting to squeeze into the morning subway at Columbus Circle. And in this city's typical bigger-than-life fashion, where else can you find half a million people shoved tightly together each December 31 to watch a giant ball descend, ringing in the New Year?

148   *Regulars, including many celebrities, crowd the front room of Elaine's, a restaurant on Second Avenue and 88th Street, which opened in 1963 (Armen Kachaturian)*

149   *Half a million souls turned out in January 1981 to cheer the returning hostages with a ticker-tape parade down Broadway (Jake Rajs)*

150–151   *Jazz at the South Street Seaport. The "Sun Ra Jet Set Omniverse Arkestra" plays for an early evening audience on Pier 16 at the Seaport—an historic district at the southern tip of Manhattan (Enrico Ferorelli)*

*152   A Chinese New Year celebration in
New York's Chinatown. The New Year is
celebrated each February with dragons,
fireworks, and music (Ken Heyman)*

152

153   Sixth Avenue and 48th Street took
on the appearance of small-town America
on the evening of the nation's Bicentennial
in 1976. Special lighting for the press
illuminates the parade at this intersection
(Dudley Gray)

154–155   Amid a Halloween celebration,
thousands make their way across Central
Park's Sheep Meadow (Stephen Green-
Armytage)

156–157   Looking down at the crowds on
Mulberry Street during the San Gennaro
Festival—an eleven-day feast in mid-
September of eating, drinking, and
religious celebration in Little Italy
(Marvin E. Newman)

158–159   New Year's Eve in Times
Square. Each year almost half a million
gather to ring in the New Year in spite
of occasional snow, sleet, and subzero
temperatures (Calvin Fentress)

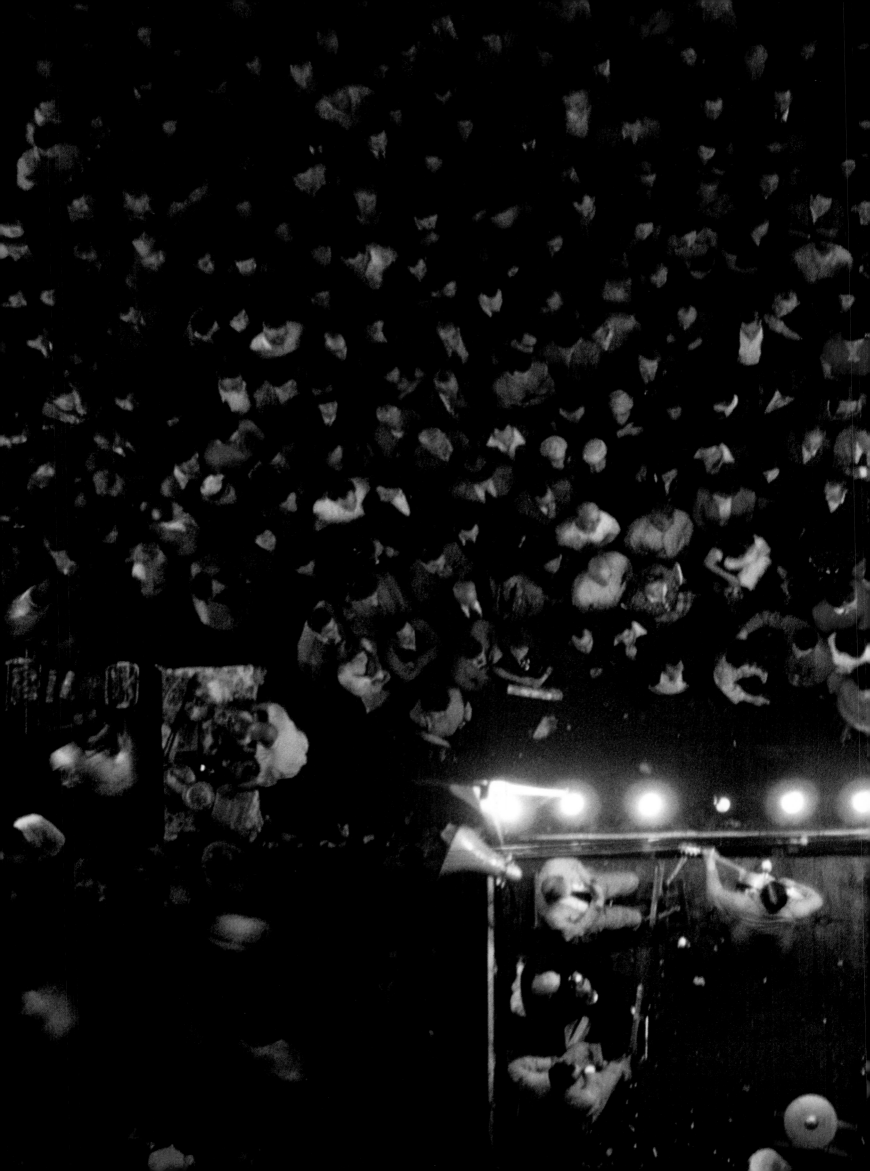

STEAM

a

b

Last year alone, Manhattan used 29,566,747,000 pounds of steam through Consolidated Edison's steam pipes. Of the five major pipes that wind beneath the streets of Manhattan—gas, electric, sewer, steam, and water—one hundred eight miles of pipes belong to the steam system. Manhattanites seem to take this phenomenon of curling whirls, of hissing blasts of steam for granted; it's the tourists who are startled and amazed by the eerie impressions sometimes created above the ground.

The first steam customer in Manhattan was a bank on Wall Street and Broadway which in 1882 ran its two elevators with steam. This was years before the multitude of small gas and electric systems merged to form the company known to most New Yorkers as Con Ed. What actually causes the steam-flows that wind their way around the city's streets? The steam that Consolidated Edison sells to office buildings for heating and air conditioning is delivered through underground pipes; the pieces of piping, although tightly connected, can at times leak. It's these leaks, along with the leaks from the city's water and sewer mains, that create a vapor of water which escapes out of the many cracks and crevices in Manhattan's streets and pavements.

160   a. Steam floats up to the color-lighted observatory of the Empire State Building on 34th Street (Hugues Colson)
       b. Steam rising from one of Manhattan's street gratings on Seventh Avenue (Hugues Colson)

161   A Consolidated Edison traffic cone on Canal Street in lower Manhattan. Beneath the streets of the city are over hundred miles of steam mains (Hugues Colson)

162   A common sight on New York's
streets—Consolidated Edison workers dig
up a section of Herald Square, an area at
the intersection of Broadway and Sixth
Avenue, and 32nd to 35th Streets. Today,
the Square is notable mainly for the
presence of Macy's and Gimbel's
department stores (Hugues Colson)

163   *A glimpse of the Empire State*
Building from a Consolidated Edison
excavation on 37th Street (Roy Morsch)

164   Midmorning in Manhattan's
garment district (extending approximately
from Sixth Avenue to Broadway and 34th
Street to 42nd Street). Steam escapes from
one of the city's manhole covers (Hugues
Colson)

165   Evening rush-hour traffic on Sixth
Avenue and 40th Street is obscured by an
ascending cloud of steam (Hugues Colson)

166–167   Late-afternoon pedestrians on
Sixth Avenue, oblivious to the swirls of
steam around them (Ernst Haas)

168–169   Lord & Taylor's Christmas
windows are an institution in New York.
The oldest surviving retail store in the city,
it was founded in 1826 (Hugues Colson)

170–171   A glimpse of Murray Hill—the
East thirties between Madison and Third
Avenues—known for its handsome
brownstones and carriage houses (Ted
Kaufman)

BROOKLYN BRIDGE

a

b

One of the most glorious landmarks in Manhattan is ironically called the Brooklyn Bridge. Initially named the East River Bridge, it was the longest suspension bridge in the world at its completion in 1883 and was considered one of the wonders of nineteenth-century America.

John Augustus Roebling, the designer of this national historic landmark, was greeted at first with incredulity when he suggested leaping across the six thousand feet of the East River with steel and cables. He died during the bridge's construction when his foot was crushed and he developed a fatal case of lockjaw. His son, Colonel Washington Roebling, took over until he, too, became ill (with a bad case of the bends) and had to supervise the final phases with the help of his wife, Emily, from his home in Brooklyn Heights. The bridge to this day is considered an awesome feat of art and engineering that has inspired poets, writers, and painters. It has evoked countless words and feelings ranging from the New York street humor in Eddie Foy's comment, "All that trouble, just to get to Brooklyn?" to the loftier sentiments put forth in Kenneth Clark's observation, "All modern New York, heroic New York, started with the Brooklyn Bridge."

172   a. The Gothic arches of pink granite flank the pedestrian walk (Bob Day)
       b. The Bridge Café at Dover Street in Manhattan in the shadow of the Brooklyn Bridge (Lorenzo D. Perrone)

173   Richard Haas' trompe l'oeil of the Brooklyn Bridge. It is painted on a Consolidated Edison substation at Peck Slip in lower Manhattan, a street that dates back to 1755 (Enrico Ferorelli)

174–175   From a pier at the Fulton Fish Market. The sun rises in New York harbor with the Brooklyn Bridge in the background (John McGrail)

176–177   A cloud of orange smoke created by a warehouse fire silhouettes the bridge (James Hamilton)

*178   Freighters, tugboats, and pleasure
craft crowd the waters beneath the bridge
(Jay Maisel)*

179   The gossamerlike cables span the
1,595.5 feet of steel across the bridge. In
1974, the metalwork was painted in the
original white-and-buff colors rather than
Public Works grey (Roy Morsch)

180–181   In Of Time and the River,
Thomas Wolfe celebrated the grandeur of
the bridge when he spoke of its "wing-like
sweep" and its "tiers of jeweled light"
(Henry Cox)

182–183   The pedestrian walk of the
Brooklyn Bridge is used by pedestrians
and bicyclists alike. Over eight hundred
bicyclists cross the bridge each day (Ted
Kaufman)

184–185   Fifty thousand watts of light
and the artistic collaboration of sculptor
Joe Strand and photographer Dudley Gray
captured this unique picture at 3:00 in the
morning (Dudley Gray)

SKIES

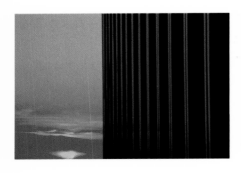

Manhattan has some of the most spectacular skies in the world. Its cloudless blue autumn days, the melancholy bleakness of its winter greys, and a sudden summer squall darkening the skies, all take on a heightened intensity against the backdrop of this incredible landscape.

Westerly winds predominate, with occasional sea breezes blowing in from the Atlantic Ocean. Autumn and spring are the invigorating seasons, while summer and winter continually surprise with their extreme and violent temperature changes. With the average New Yorker breathing in about thirty-five pounds of air each day, the quality of our atmosphere becomes a crucial matter. Sulfur dioxide, carbon monoxide, smoke, dust, and nitrogen dioxide all crowd the skies, enhancing the color of our city's sunsets, but corroding our buildings, our parks, and our lungs.

186   A red sun sets over lower Manhattan (John Scheiber)

187   The Empire State Building glistens below a cloudy early evening sky (Jean-Pierre Pappis)

188   *A montage of water tanks outlined against the West Side at dusk (Ted Kaufman)*

189   A solitary nude on a rooftop in Soho
faces east as a summer sun sets in the west
(Dudley Gray)

190–191   The needle of the Guardian
Life Insurance Building, next to 200 Park
Avenue South, thrusts toward a grey sky
above Union Square, the intersection of
Park Avenue South and Broadway, and
14th to 17th Street (Joseph Vasta)

192–193   An explosion of clouds and
setting sun above 23rd Street and Tenth
Avenue on the West Side (Dudley Gray)

194–195   The lights of lower Manhattan
glow as a pier fire on the New Jersey shore
rages out of control and helicopters streak
overhead (Paul Elson)

196   *Looking north on the Hudson*
River as a summer storm approaches
Manhattan. Thunder, lightning, and
heavy rains envelop Riverside Park in the
foreground (Walter Iooss, Jr.)

197   *From a Central Park West apartment vantage point, a peach mist settles over Sheep Meadow in Central Park and the East Side skyline (Ruth Orkin)*

198–199   *A sun-worshiping cyclist takes advantage of a cloudless blue sky and a trafficless West Side Highway, which has become a haven for joggers and bicyclists since it was closed to traffic on December 15, 1973. The towers of Independence Plaza, a residential apartment building constructed in 1975, on the right, and the Hudson River piers flank the decaying highway (Michael George)*

SPEED

a

b

Manhattan, a 24-hour-a-day city, is electric energy at rest and in motion. Perhaps nowhere else in the world is there as much going on, stepping out, and moving around the clock. It's a hyperactive city that's grown up in a rush. Everywhere pedestrians, cars, bicyclists, and joggers jam the streets. Even the subways never stop, offering subterranean movement night and day at speeds of up to forty miles an hour.

Urban observer William Whyte, in his study on street life in New York, discovered that New Yorkers are extremely fast walkers. The men he watched averaged between 250–275 feet a minute and they rarely bumped into one another. But Whyte goes on: "It's the out-of-towners who give them the trouble, with their maddening slowness, their ambiguous moves, their tendency to walk 3 and 4 abreast, sauntering and dawdling. It's like playing against an inferior opponent and throws New Yorkers off their game."

200 a. One of two thousand meals a day rushed to a table by one of the sixty waiters employed at Christmas time at Luchow's Restaurant on 14th Street opposite Irving Place (Paul Elson)

b. A tugboat in the harbor of lower Manhattan. Documented tugboats and ocean liners are exempt from speed limit restrictions placed on registered pleasure craft in New York harbor (Laszlo Hege)

201 A taxi zooms past the entrance of Radio City Music Hall at Sixth Avenue and 50th Street. Legal speed limit on most Manhattan streets is 30 M.P.H. (John E. Barrett)

202   One of New York's estimated eight
thousand daily bicyclists in midtown
Manhattan maneuvers through downtown
traffic on Broadway. Legal speed limit for
bicycles is the same as that for cars—30
M.P.H. or the posted speed (Ted Kaufman)

203   A lone jogger on the path that
overlooks Manhattan's billion-gallon
reservoir in Central Park. The path, a
haven for runners and nature walkers, is
1.5 miles around. A good jogger can run
it in fifteen minutes (Jere Cockrell)

204   There are 6,500 subway cars in New
York City. Cruising speed for the R-46 cars
is 30–40 M.P.H. but they can reach 70
M.P.H. (Aram Gesar)

*205   Taxi traffic at 43rd Street and Ninth
Avenue with the Empire State Building
in the distance. There are over eleven
thousand medallion cabs in New York City
(Brian Lav)*

*206   A private plane maneuvers through
the Twin Towers of the World Trade
Center—thirteen hundred fifty feet of
sheer uninterrupted steel and glass and
separated by a distance of one hundred
thirty feet. The speed limit for all aircraft
flying ten thousand feet or less above
Manhattan is 250 knots (Peter B. Kaplan)*

*207   With lower Manhattan in the
background, the S.S. Norway, formerly
the France, visits New York harbor on its
maiden voyage under its new guise. The
Norway weighs sixty-nine thousand five
hundred pounds and cruises at sixteen to
eighteen knots, although her top speed is
twenty-one knots (John McGrail)*

REFLECTIONS

a

b

c

Manhattan abounds in reflected images. The city's dazzling array of glass-covered buildings, shiny steel facades, elaborate store windows, painstakingly buffed limousine tops, and even, at times, its mud puddles create a potpourri of reflections so subtle that sometimes only the camera's eye can catch them.

Nowhere else can one see so many incredible juxtapositions as here—stately old buildings mirrored in their more modern counterparts, cube structures wrinkled in curving glass facades, and an anonymous kaleidoscope of faces bouncing off taxicab windows.

When night falls, the city's reflections turn brassier as the flashing fluorescent lights of Times Square and the endless river of cars and taxis on the main avenues of Manhattan create a white-and-red glow in the city's glass towers.

208   a. A vision of clouds in a window on Wall Street (Jan Cobb)

b. The Flatiron Building as seen in a puddle in Madison Square Park (Frank Spinelli)

c. A glimpse of the Empire State Building in a crosstown bus (Chris Collins)

209   A reflection, atop a car's hood, of the Solomon R. Guggenheim Museum, built in 1959 on upper Fifth Avenue by Frank Lloyd Wright. The museum is one of Wright's final works and one of his most controversial (Jake Rajs)

210   The curving stainless-steel exterior of the Market Diner on West Street. The diner, a favorite haunt of taxicab drivers since 1921, is open twenty-four hours a day,
seven days a week (Hugues Colson)

211   The lights of Rockefeller Center's Christmas tree are mirrored on the lacquered hood of a Phantom Rolls-Royce limousine (Hugues Colson)

212   The stately Plaza Hotel, built in 1907 and forming New York's first public urban plaza, shimmers in the windows of Hugh Hefner's Playboy Club on 59th Street (Jon Ortner)

213   The southern facade of Grand Central Terminal is reflected in the glass-enclosed walls of the Hyatt Regency Hotel on Lexington Avenue and 42nd Street (Peter B. Kaplan)

214   The east side of Madison Avenue is
reflected in the display window of Sotheby Parke Bernet, the auction house at 980 Madison Avenue (Frank Spinelli)

215   The Metropolitan Opera House in its new form was designed by Wallace K. Harrison and opened in September 1966 with the production of Samuel Barber's Antony and Cleopatra. Focal point of the Lincoln Center complex, it contains seven rehearsal halls and has scenery space for fifteen operas (Sonja Bullaty)

216–217   Eighty thousand faces a year pass in front of the three hundred forty-eight mirrored panels at the Georgette Klinger Skin Care Salon at 501 Madison Avenue, where men and women flock for facials and treatments. Tip Sempliner designed the main salon in 1975 (Dudley Gray)

RED

a

b

c

In a city of granites and greys, the color red commands immediate attention. The constant visual bombardment that afflicts New Yorkers from all sides makes red stand out whether it be the red light of a traffic signal, a red hat, a red truck, the red safety strip of a bicycle at dusk, or the relentless flashing red neon of an all-night saloon.

Without a doubt, Manhattan's most glamorous red is the red of its sunsets. Yet there is a decidedly unromantic explanation for this occurrence and that is, simply, the dirtier the air, the redder the sunrises and sunsets. Of the seven colors that make up the white light of sunlight, scientists tell us, the short wave lengths (at one end of the rainbow—the blues and violets) are stopped by the particles of dust and chemical emissions in the air, while the longer wave lengths (at the opposite end—the reds and oranges) tend to get through, giving us the vivid red skies.

Whatever the reason, the ultimate effect of this phenomenon is the pinkish haze that softens and bathes the sharp grey edges of this city.

218 *a. Hell's Kitchen, a restaurant in the area that bears its name—formerly a notorious section of the city in the forties and fifties west of Seventh Avenue (Roy Morsch)*

b. A mannequin in a shop window at Madison Avenue and 68th Street— a neighborhood of elegant shops and boutiques (Eleni Mylonas)

c. A New York City fireman in his red truck. In a typical year, firemen respond to over sixty-eight thousand calls, as many as twenty-six thousand of them false alarms (Peter B. Kaplan)

219 *The afternoon sun on the red brick facade of a building on Perry Street in Greenwich Village (Michael George)*

220   Bright red pumps cross the
esplanade of the Chase Manhattan Plaza,
located in downtown Manhattan on
William Street (Henry Cox)

221　A woman boarding the 86th Street
crosstown bus at Central Park West. In a
twenty-four hour period, approximately
seventy crosstown trips are made (Susan
Lazarus)

222–223　Red-clad Radio City Music
Hall Rockettes film an "I Love New York"
commercial in Rockefeller Center. An
institution since 1932, the thirty-six
Rockettes are renowned for their high
kickline finales (Roy Morsch)

224　On certain days, due to a
combination of factors including the
weather, the time of year, and the intensity
of the sunset, the Empire State Building
assumes a reddish hue for about one
minute (Hugues Colson) ...

225　...And on certain other days, due to
man-made forces, the top seventy-two to
one hundred two floors of the Empire
State Building can glow red, yellow, blue,
green...whatever. This procedure can take
up to three days since it is done completely
by hand as different colored gels are
placed in sleeves around the exterior of the
building (Peter B. Kaplan)

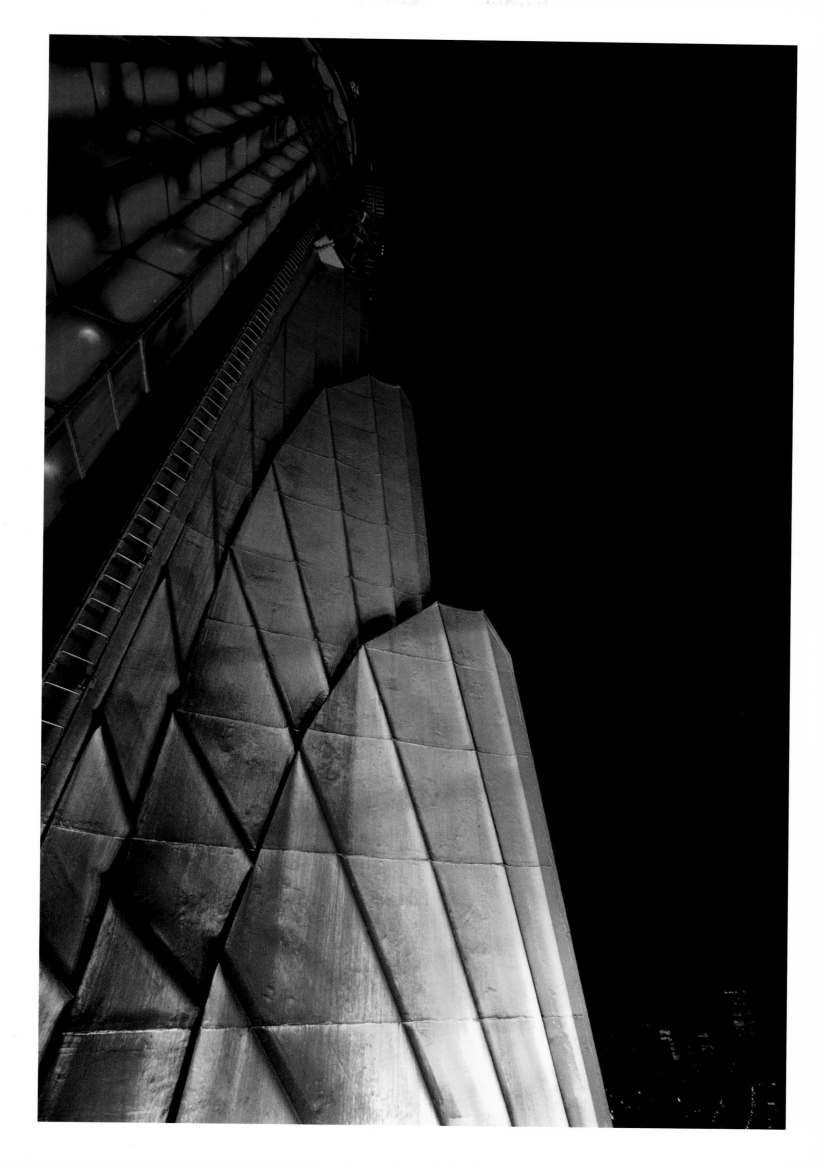

VISITORS

a

b

c

Each year, over seventeen million people come to visit Manhattan, making it one of the largest tourist attractions in the world. Some are silently whisked by limousine from Kennedy Airport to the Helmsley Palace and their seven-hundred-dollar suite, while others arrive by Greyhound bus, hoping to find some inexpensive lodging at a youth hostel in Greenwich Village or Tribeca.

Whatever their circumstances, Manhattan is a great equalizer in terms of tasting its pleasures. The view from the 102nd floor of the Empire State Building, a draft beer at McSorley's Old Ale House, a boat ride in the lake at Central Park, and just plain walking around this marvelous city are pleasures available to both the well-heeled and the more penurious traveler on a package tour.

Manhattan has a way of gracefully accommodating its seventeen million visitors in much the same fashion it has assimilated new-comers over the years—they seem to blend into the rhythm of the city.

226 a. One of the trains belonging to the performers of the Ringling Brothers and Barnum & Bailey Circus, temporarily parked under the West Side Highway (Jane Schreibman)

b. A face in the crowd on St. Patrick's Day (Thomas A. Kelly)

c. Mickey Mouse awaits the start of Macy's Thanksgiving Day Parade (Stephanie L. Marcus)

227 Two visiting monks viewing Manhattan from the observation deck at the World Trade Center (Timothy Eagan)

228 *The Bandoleros Band from
Northbrook High School in Houston,
Texas, passes in front of Macy's, the world's
largest department store, at its annual
Thanksgiving Day Parade, an institution
since 1924 (John Scheiber)*

229   The RCA Building's observation deck—at sixty-five stories high one of the city's great vantage points—affords these French sailors a crisp autumnal view of Manhattan (Henri Dauman)

230–231   Hours before the Macy's Thanksgiving Day Parade will climax in front of the famous department store, members from the Elko High School Band of Elko, Nevada, take it easy on Manhattan's upper West Side (Mariette Pathy Allen)

232–233   Clowns from Macy's department store mingle with spectators at the start of the Thanksgiving Day Parade at Central Park West and 77th Street. Over half a million people, one third of them out-of-towners, line the streets of Manhattan to catch a glimpse of the parade (Mark Ivins)

234   Finishers wrapped in space blankets
at the New York City Marathon, which
now encompasses all five boroughs of the
city. Begun in 1970, with a field of one
hundred twenty-six starters and seventy-
two finishers, the race is now one of the
world's largest and is open to world class
and amateur runners alike (John McGrail)

235   The most prestigious dog show in
the country is the Westminster Kennel Club
Dog Show, held annually in February
since 1877 at Madison Square Garden.
Here French bulldogs compete for best of
breed (Stephen Green-Armytage)

WATER TANKS

a

b

To most New Yorkers, water tanks appear to be anachronisms—quaint towers settled among the city's cubes and slick structures. They are certainly a reminder of a more gentle architectural period in our environs, but even today these towers still serve some necessary and life-saving purposes. In case of a burning building, they feed water into the sprinkler and standpipe systems, allowing firemen safe exit from the building; they can also supply drinking and washing water.

Usually made of redwood, a natural insulator, or occasionally of metal, these 5,000 to 25,000 gallon towers have been a visible part of the Manhattan skyline since the 1900s. In fact, when Francis Ford Coppola was shooting the movie *Godfather II* on East 6th Street, he had his stagehands construct a false tank of masonite atop one of the street's tenements to give it a more realistic New York feeling.

Because water pressure can only rise so high in most buildings and apartment houses, the water from the city main is pumped into the water tank by means of a pump activated by a float switch whenever the water is down one-third of its total supply.

Tanks are found on almost all buildings over seven stories (some have pumps and pressure tanks built in the basement or on various floors) and if they're not always visible to the naked eye, it's only because of the elaborate boxes and battlements that architects sometimes construct around them in a losing effort to disguise them.

236   a. Workmen repair a water tank at 121 Madison Avenue (Serge Hambourg)
b. A tank in the historic Chelsea district (Roy Morsch)

237   The side of an apartment building dwarfs a water tank on 12th Street between University Place and Broadway (Timothy Eagan)

238   Looking west at a setting sun above 33rd Street (Bill Farrell)

239   A lone tank on Chambers Street in lower Manhattan. In pre-Civil War years this area was considered daringly uptown (Sonja Bullaty)

240   Clouds of steam rising on a
Christmas day over the tanks and the
tops of apartment towers on 88th Street
(Charles E. Dorris)

241   Set in the heart of Manhattan's
antique district at 12th Street between
University Place and Broadway, two water
tanks are defined against the sky
(Timothy Eagan)

242–243   The roof of a water tower
on 85th Street and West End Avenue
foreshadows the Empire State Building
(Margery Motzkin)

LOOKING DOWN

Most connoisseurs of the city's architectural pleasures would undoubtedly recommend a look skyward to get a true feeling of this city. But Manhattan's real aficionados know that there are constant visual surprises to be found just by looking down and not all of them need be from observation decks and rooftops.

Stroll to the top of the ramp at the Solomon R. Guggenheim Museum and look down at the quarter mile of spiraling marble-and-concrete walk; stop in at 220 East 42nd Street, at the Art Deco lobby of the Daily News Building, and gaze below at the four-thousand-pound globe, recessed into the floor, that makes a complete revolution every ten minutes; or look down from almost any window to the cityscape below to experience the pulsating and changing street life of Manhattan.

244   The smallest piece of real estate in Manhattan measures 24 x 24 x 26 inches and is located in front of the Village Smoke Shop at Seventh Avenue and Sheridan Square in Greenwich Village (John McGrail)

245   The Ward's Island Pedestrian Bridge over the East River was painted red and blue in 1976 and has since faded to shades of purple and pink. It connects Manhattan with Ward's Island, formerly farm land and now occupied by a sewage disposal plant, a state hospital, and a small park (Peter B. Kaplan)

246   Half a million people pass each day through Grand Central Terminal at 42nd Street and Park Avenue. Underneath the terminal are some thirty-three miles of tracks on two levels (Peter B. Kaplan)

247   The enormous spinning globe dominates the lobby of the Daily News Building at 220 East 42nd Street. The newspaper's Manhattan edition is actually printed in this building. The name of the paper was changed to the Daily Planet when the movie Superman was shot in and around the building (Peter B. Kaplan)

248–249   Eleven A.M. on the floor of the New York Stock Exchange on Broad Street in the city's financial district. The price of a seat fluctuates, but approximately $200,000 will buy you one on the Exchange, where one thousand five hundred different stocks are at times traded (Marvin E. Newman)

250 *The spiraling staircase in the*
seventeen-story landmark Ansonia Hotel
at Broadway and 74th Street. The hotel
was finished in 1904, and its three-foot
thick, virtually soundproof walls have
made it a haven over the years for
musicians, among them Caruso, Menuhin,
Stravinsky, and Toscanini (Henri Dauman)

251 *Frank Lloyd Wright's spiral ramp*
in the Solomon R. Guggenheim Museum
measures over a quarter of a mile (Sonja
Bullaty)

252 *A flower vendor peddles his red, green, and yellow bouquets beneath the Helmsley Building on Park Avenue (Peter B. Kaplan)*

253   Ten stories down from a Central
Park West window, a Manhattan street is
beaded with raindrops (Tom Zimberoff)

254–255   Mickey Mouse, nine thousand
five hundred cubic feet of helium and
standing fifty-seven feet tall, glides past
some of the spectators that line the route of
Macy's Thanksgiving Day Parade
(Ruth Orkin)

LIST OF PHOTOGRAPHERS

All photographs are copyrighted in the following photographers' names:

FIRST EDITION

George Grosz photographs: Estate of George Grosz, Princeton, N.J.
Courtesy of Kimmel/Cohn Photography Arts
Special thanks to The Museum of the City of New York

Library of Congress Catalog Card Number: 81-66740
International Standard Book Number: 0-8109-1311-9
© *1981 J.-C. Suarès*

Published in 1981 by Harry N. Abrams, Incorporated, New York
All rights reserved. No part of the contents of this book may be
reproduced without the written permission of the publishers

Printed and bound in Japan